Candy Cane
CHRISTMAS

Helen Haidle
Illustrated by Rick Incrocci

The text of this book may be sung to the
tune of *"Jesus Loves Me."*

CPH.
Concordia Publishing House

To my third- and fourth-grade Sunday school students during 1995 and 1996. You touched my heart as you shared the candy cane and its message in your classrooms, with teammates, with neighbors . . . and even with playground bullies!

$\mathcal{D}$o you know the story of
Candy canes and God's great love;
Why we celebrate His birth,
And why Jesus came to earth?

*O*nce there lived a candy man
Who designed a special plan;

Mixed and cooked a tasty treat
That could tell a story sweet.

Candy canes can tell us all,
Of God's Son, born weak and small,

Jesus—God's dear gift of love,
Sent to earth from heaven above.

*C*andy canes look like a "*J*"—
"*J*" for Jesus, born this day.

Jesus — it's a wondrous name,
Savior from all sin and shame.

$\mathcal{D}$on't chew candy canes—just lick!
They are solid, *rock-hard* sticks!

Jesus is my *ROCK*, my friend.
On His love I can depend.

*C*andy canes were first made *white,*
'Cause the baby born that night

Was the pure and holy One,
Spotless Lamb, God's only Son.

*J*esus lived and died for you;
Now you're pure and holy too!

He will cleanse your heart from sin,
And help you to trust in Him.

*I*t's a *shepherd's staff* you see.
My Good Shepherd cares for me.

I am weak, but He is strong.
He will rescue me from wrong.

With a cane to tend their sheep,
Shepherds guard and safely keep

Little lambs like me from harm,
I am safe in Jesus' arms.

Stripes on candy canes are *red,*
Like the blood that Jesus shed.

See the scars and wounds He bore.
See the crown of thorns He wore.

One big stripe reminds us all
Of the wooden cross so tall,

Lifting Jesus high above,
As He stretched His arms in love.

When you give your gifts away,
Laugh and sing this Christmas Day.

Share a box of candy canes;
Tell the world that Jesus reigns!

THE MEANING OF THE CANDY CANE

Hard Candy – reminds us that we can depend on Jesus, our solid *Rock*.

White Candy – reminds us that Jesus, the *holy Son of God washes us white as snow.*

"J" shape – J is for the precious *name of JESUS,* our Savior.

Shepherd's staff – Helps us remember that Jesus is our *Good Shepherd.*

Small red stripes – Remind us of Jesus' blood. He *suffered* and *died* for our sin.

One large red stripe – Reminds us of the *cross* on which Jesus was crucified.